Online Marketing Strategies to

Grow Your Business

Disclaimer:

This work may not be copied, sold, used as content in any manner without sufficient rights to sell or distribute it as your own. It must be used solely for the purpose of growing and expanding your practice.

Every effort has been made to be accurate in this publication. The publisher does not assume any responsibility for errors, omissions or contrary interpretation. We do our best to provide the best information on the subject of local marketing, but just reading it does not guarantee success. You will need to apply every step of the process in order to get the results you are looking for.

This publication is not intended for use as a source of any legal advice. The information contained in this guide may be subject to laws in the United States and other jurisdictions. We suggest carefully reading the necessary terms of the services/products used before applying it to any activity which is, or may be, regulated. We do not assume any responsibility for what you choose to do with this information. Use your own judgment.

Some examples of past results are used in this publication; they are intended to be for example purposes only and do not guarantee you will get the same results. Your results may differ from ours. Your results from the use of this information will depend on you, your skills and effort, and other different unpredictable factors.

It is important for you to clearly understand that all marketing activities carry the possibility of loss of investment for testing purposes. Use this information wisely and at your own risk.

Contents

LOCAL MARKETING
MADE SIMPLE

Getting Started

What is Local Online Marketing?

Local online marketing generally refers to any online marketing techniques that a local business, in any industry, uses to market itself online to the area it operates in.

Local marketing is mostly used by small businesses like stores and restaurants but professionals – think doctors, dentists, lawyers, and accountants, also use local marketing to promote themselves around their specific location.

A local company or a business that pulls in customers from the local area uses specific strategies to engage new and potential customers related to their specific community. Transferring that same marketing activity to the online marketing world can easily surpass the results achieved with offline marketing.

A huge percentage of customers search online to learn about products and services. According to a recent study, 75% of Internet

users perform local searches on a regular basis; more than 100 million people a month use Google Maps from mobile phones, 66% of Americans use online local search to locate businesses, and 82% of local searches follow up offline via an in-store visit, phone call or purchase. Those companies can complement their offline business strategies with highly effective online marketing strategies.

Local Online Marketing provides you with the ability to understand your customer's behaviors and purchasing habits because you can know more about online customers through web-based tracking (Google Analytics) than you can know just by their coming into your store.

You can use online channels like your website, mobile applications, social media, local search and emails to attract local customers. When used in the correct combination, online marketing drives tangible results and builds meaningful businesses.

Local marketing is an ongoing process instead of a single campaign or event that will end after a fixed time. If you have the correct approach and do it right, it will always give you a positive return on your marketing investment.

How is Local Marketing generally used on the web?

In the online marketing world you can use online marketing strategies to do local marketing, build brand awareness in your local area and generate tangible leads that convert into paying customers – many of them long-term.

It's all about how you reach, know, and interact with your audience in a meaningful way, driving behavior in the form of inquiries and purchases. Here are a few online media channels normally used to target local audiences.

Website: Local customers normally get excited when their favorite store or provider has a website showing their products and services. It's a lot easier for a customer to research, choose, and select with the use of a web page.

Having a very informative and updated website will be a great help to your target audience as well. The majority of people prefer to fill out an inquiry form instead of calling or speaking to someone. Giving them multiple contact opportunities through your website can go a long way in connecting with your customers and prospects.

Social Media: People hang out a lot more on social media networks than on a website, and that's where you should establish your local presence. Businesses who do this well generate local customers and

referrals. Building a social presence is now easier than ever even if its still new to you.

The number of followers, likes, shares, reviews, comments, retweets and any other social action shows the level of interest your audience has in your products and services. Responding to and engaging with social media users is a good way to show that you care about your audience and business.

Local Search: Is your website listed by location and the local market it serves? Are the keywords and descriptions you use for search engines chosen by the people searching for a business like yours in a specific area, for example 'Lawyer in Mainport' or 'Fishing Store in Brunswick'?

Even as a marketing practitioner, I still find it both exciting and scary that you can target your audience directly with the use of Local search engines, pay-per-click marketing, and social promotion. *And the great thing is that just a few of your local competitors know about it or how to do it effectively,* which puts you in a unique position to "steal" their customers or simply improve market share by using online marketing techniques.

LOCAL MARKETING
MADE SIMPLE

Local Lead Generation: I have seen how Cost-Per-Action (CPA) websites offer you $10 to $20 for every new lead generated they generate. But in our training we will show you how to generate leads for your business without relying on a third party. In fact, showing you how to get quality leads for free and/or at very low cost is one of the purposes of this guide. Knowledge is a powerful thing.

Having local customers in a contact list that you develop is a form of lead generation and one of the greatest opportunities you have for growing your business. In additional to lead generation we'll show you how to build a list you can market to again and again.

Why Local Marketing?

Local marketing is the most efficient ways to use your budget when targeting prospective customers from a specific geographic area (ex: within 20 miles of your location). By focusing your marketing dollars on reaching those most likely to visit your store or purchase your products and services, you're making marketing dollars work harder for you and producing better results.

In addition to getting more from your marketing budget, local marketing has many additional benefits. Here are a few to consider:

Credibility: Having a powerful local presence on the web will increase your business' authenticity and brand recognition.

If you place your business on the web with images, physical address and valuable information about your services, viewers will rely on

local listings more than traditional listings (ex: yellow pages).

According to an NDA Group report, about 57% of online customers browse and research online, but purchase offline.

Stronger Access to Local Market: You can take advantage of local marketing by having a direct connection with your customers and community. This maximizes your chances to gain additional opportunities for exposure, growing your presence throughout the community.

Brand Loyalty: A really high level of customer service and the creation of top quality solutions will help you build your brand in the local community. Make sure to offer quality products and provide the best services to your local customers who will provide referrals,

share their experience on social media, and return to make future purchases.

Targeting and Personalization: You can get extremely targeted customers for your products and services because online data helps you reach them locally - understanding who they are, where they come from and what they like. This makes targeting much more efficient and highly effective.

You can classify customers on their demographic profile like age, gender, buying habits, geographic location, income level, occupation, hobbies and interests. You can do almost anything on the web to find and promote your services to those most likely to buy.

Increase revenue: How much do you usually spend on local marketing activities around your target area? How much business do you think you can get by doing similar marketing online and with just a few clicks?

The principal of targeting a lot more of your potential customers at the point when they are searching for the types of services you offer not only makes sense but provides a much higher return on your investment. In fact, online marketing outperforms traditional

advertising as much as 20 to 1. I don't know about you but I want my marketing dollars producing new customers for my business.

Here are some amazing eye opening facts that will show you why you have to use Local Marketing to market your Business (stats by SM Digital)

- 74% of Internet users perform local searches.
- More than 100 MILLION PEOPLE a month use Google Maps from mobile phones to find business information.
- 66% of American's use online local search, like Google local search to locate local businesses.
- 61% of local searches result in purchases.
- 54% of Americans have substituted the internet and local search for phone books.
- 82% of local searches follow up offline via an in-store visit, phone call or purchase.
- As much as 62% of Google Search traffic has local content.

Data like this makes it clear there is a lot of money to be made with Local Marketing. And while lots of people might be talking about it, very few can really teach you how to productively use Local Marketing to grow your business.

Lesson 1: Local Online Directories

Local online marketing has changed radically thanks to the redevelopment of local online directories. Think online yellow pages on steroids. In the past, many websites were developed to simply list companies, products, websites, and other online resources. Over time, Google started penalizing these sites because they were pretty much un-usable and often considered link-farms. In typical Google fashion they turned this around and built a verifiable database of businesses, giving birth to a new era of online directories, reviews, and in-depth information about all types of local businesses.

As Google moved into the development of verified online directories, a whole new industry of local directories emerged. In a technical sense we call these online directories 'data aggregators'. The concept is pretty simple. Create a verified online listing of local businesses and show these listing to individuals searching via their mobile devices. Users will see results based on proximity to location as well as other factors such as completeness of listing, reviews, and other criteria. You see this all the time but probably never thought about it. Searching for anything business related on your mobile

devices usually returns a result from the Google or other high profile data aggregators.

What you probably didn't know

Although Google has the largest directory of online businesses on the planet, they use multiple sources to verify their data (i.e. data aggregators). In the US there are four major data aggregators. If you get your business listed in these 4, you'll show up in more local searches with more information about your business than some of your competitors. They are: *Infogroup, Acxiom, Localeze and Factual.* In a little bit, I'll show you how to get your business listed on these and other local directories and how to dominate local search results in your area.

The reason why online local directories and data aggregators are driving local search results is because of the concept of local intent. Google assumes, based on their data which show that 60% of searches are for local businesses, that many of the searches coming from a mobile device are local. People tend to seek solutions to their problems and needs by proximity. For example, if you need a new grill you're probably not getting on a plane to buy a new one. Rather, you're looking for a store close to you that sells a variety of grills. In Google's wisdom, they are pre-filtering results based on

location, only returning results listed in their directory or other local search directories that meet certain criteria. Results are continually updated so that searchers receive the best available information for making a buying decision.

Getting Listed in Local Online Directories

Once you understand the importance of local online directories the next step is to learn the most effective strategy for getting listed and giving your business the best chance of showing up in search results when individuls pull out their mobile phones.

Mastering the online local marketing game starts with Google's online directory, **"Google My Business"** and promoting your local business through the data aggregators I mentioned above. The good news is that tools are available for distributing your information to the largest data aggregators and keeping your information updated to ensure the highest possible ranking. I'll be discussing each of these tools in the lessons that follow. For now, it's important to realize that getting your business listed in the Google directory is paramount to promoting your business online and using a data aggregator is equally important if you want prospective customers seeing your business and considering you as their provider of choice.

Lesson 2: Google My Business

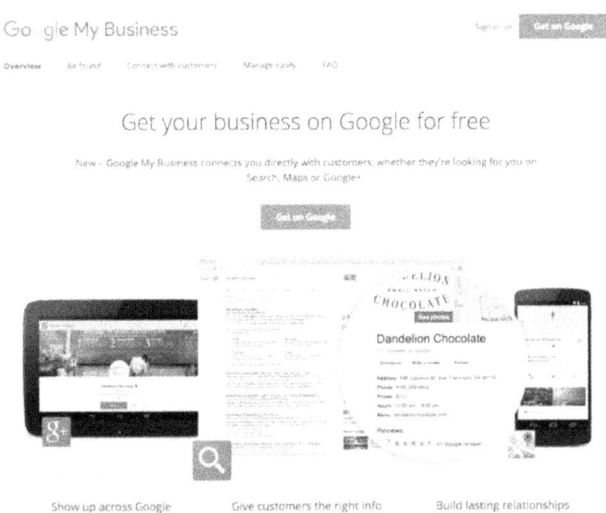

Google operates the largest local business directory online called Google My Business. It has had a number of different names over time, but is still the most important local directory available today.

Google My Business consists of a multi-layer platform which connects you directly with customers, whether they're looking for you on Google Search, Google Maps or Google+.

To get your business listed on this directory, you need to create a Google My Business Account which is free, simply by clicking on the "Get on Google" button. Of course, you'll need to have a Gmail account already created to have access to this service.

If you've already created any Google Maps or Google Places accounts, login with the same details and make sure everything is updated. If you do not have a Gmail account, set up takes less than two minutes and is self-explanatory. Simply navigate to accounts.google.com to sign up.

Once logged into Google My Business, you will able to create a new profile. Google will evaluate your current location and ask you to search their directory to see if a listing already exists.

After searching, you will be able to set up your profile by choosing your Business Type and submitting your business name. Assuming you don't find your business listed, which probably is the case, you can click on "Let me enter the full business details".

Next, you'll submit your Business information with all the information requested. The best recommendation is to complete as much of the information as possible. The more information you submit, the better your online presence.

After entering your location or profile information, you will be asked if you are authorized to manage this business and if you agree to the terms of service.

Then you'll need to verify your business via a verification code that will be sent to the postal address you have just inserted into your Business Information.

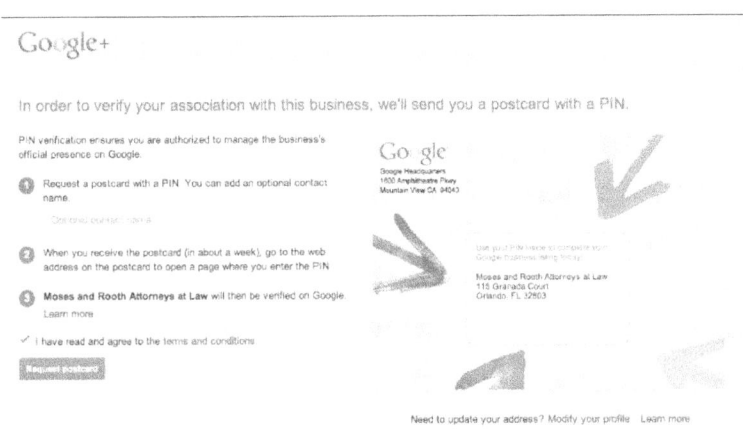

It usually takes 2 weeks to receive a verification post card in the mail. **THIS FINAL PIECE IS EXTREMELY IMPORTANT.** Once you receive the verification pin (via postcard) you MUST return to Google My Business and enter the pin number. Your post card will have the specific URL to visit online and enter your code. Once you enter the required verification code, your listing will be confirmed

and will start appearing in less than 72 hours for local online searches.

Let me give you a number of very important pieces of advice to consider while you are setting up your Google My Business account.

The first is that you must submit all information Google asks you enter throughout the sign up process. Inside your Google's Business Page dashboard, by clicking on Edit, you will be able to add a lot more important information - you must add every single thing there, too.

We strongly advise you to use 100% accurate information, you must use your real Business name (not a keyword), updated business address, real contact info, your actual business hours, real business picture and a really professional and descriptive introduction, etc.

Secondly, we advise you to check if there are other Google Business Pages for the exact same practice. Clicking on the settings you will be able to see all pages listed, just go inside of the duplicated one, click on edit, and going down you will find the "Delete this Page" link.

Finally, it's important that you know the principal Ranking Factors of your Google Business Page. They include:

- Accurate and Optimized Business Information: all of your business information should be completely filled in and accurate in all places: Google Products, Website, Local Listings, etc.

- Reviews: reviews are an extremely important feature Google My Business is offering as well. Google organizes reviews by score as well, and besides registering these reviews inside of Google's platform, Google has also the ability to retrieve and store those reviews from other websites. Something that is offering real value to other people will surely be picked up by Google to be on top.

- Post Frequencies: consistent updates to your profile will tell people your business is alive and that you are always trying to offer new content to your audience.

- Real Followers: the greater the number of real followers from your local area your business has the higher the ranking potential your business will get for that same audience related to your local business.

- Followers Engagement: another sign of being alive is your followers' engagement. There is no point having a great deal of real followers for your local business listing if no one is having real and constant interaction with your business.

- Citations: with this we mean that your NAP (Local Business Name, Local Business Address and your Local Business Phone number) should be everywhere on the web. Make sure it is consistent with what you have on the website. Even small deviations can negatively impact your ranking. Make sure your address in Google My Business is exactly the same as what you have on your website.

Lesson 3: Moz Local

Once you've submitted your business information and verified your listing on Google My Business, the next step is to make sure your business information appears on each of the four major data aggregators.

MOZ Local is designed for businesses who want to distribute their information to the leading data aggregators and improve their local online listings. With MOZ Local you can easily manage your online listing, all you need to do is upload your business information with a few clicks and it notifies you if any issues arise. This is a single point solution for making sure your business information appears in large portion of local search results.

You can establish a consistent business listing in directories and popular websites with MOZ Local. MOZ Local shows you when information has been submitted and any issues you may have with duplicate listings.

The Category Research tool of MOZ Local helps you choose the right search engine categories for your local business and provides transparent reports of your listings. It is the only self-service location data management software that lists your local business with all major U.S. data aggregators. Make sure categories reflect your core business. It's better to be accurate than have multiple categories that aren't reflective of what you do or the products you sell.

Lesson 4: Yext

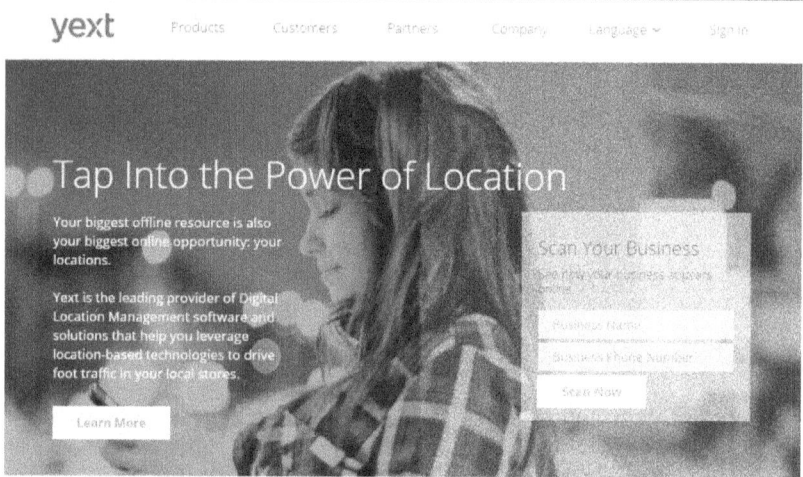

If your customers don't find you when they search online via a desktop computer or mobile device, you might as well not exist. After getting listed on Google My Business, the next step is to submit your information to data aggregators (ex: Moz Local). But don't stop there. If you want to dominate the online space, you need to submit your business information through multiple channels.

Yext is an all-in-one location based online marketing platform for local businesses that distributes your information to some data aggregators and top online directories. Business listing management helps you discover where your business is listed online, identifies

the gaps and gives you significant local search coverage. It also identifies inaccuracies or inconsistencies and fixes them with a site by site review and one-click override.

Yext stands out from some of the other local directory solutions due to their robust user interface, allowing you to upload and distribute expanded business listings. Yext also monitors reviews across various review sites.

Lesson 5: Yelp

Yelp is a powerful resource for professionals of all types. Many of the people I work with always question my Yelp recommendation if they've never listed their business on Yelp before. This is because of the misnomer that Yelp is only for restaurants — nothing could be further from the truth. Yelp is one of the largest directories of small

and medium sized business on the planet (next to Google). It provides user reviews and recommendations of top restaurants, shopping, professional services and more. Don't underestimate its value. Many of the stores, retailers, doctors, and accountants we've consulted for generate 2-5 new customers per week from Yelp.

When it comes to Yelp and online reviews, many businesses start to immediately think about all of the customer issues they've hand in the past and whether or not they'll be saddled with bad online reviews. Due to this concern I've focused a whole chapter on Reviews and how to manage them.

Lesson 6: Reviews

Reviews are an essential part of doing business online. When it comes to online marketing, favorable reviews are worth their weight in gold and serve to strengthen your brand. According to a recent study more than 69% of online customers rely on reviews to make buying decisions.

Unfortunately, not all reviews are positive. But despite popular belief negative reviews can be your ally. In this section I'm going to

discuss the role that reviews play in your business, explain how to get positive reviews, and what to do when negative reviews happen.

No business is perfect - so expecting to receive only positive reviews can be a bit naive. Not to worry though. As someone who has worked with thousands of businesses who needed to fight back against negative online content, I'll share some best practices for minimizing negative reviews and making negative reviews work in your favor.

While you can't stop negative reviews from happening, it's not the bad reviews themselves, but how you deal with them that determine the impact they have on your business. Here's a little secret. One of the most effective ways to reduce the impact of negative reviews is to increase the number of positive reviews your business received online. If a single tree falls in a forest among thousands, it will largely go unnoticed.

Something to consider is that many customers aren't interested in leaving reviews. In fact, getting customers to write reviews can be a challenging task. However, if you ask customers the right way, you'll be able to find those willing to leave positive feedback. Businesses that are overly persistent run the risk of upsetting customers who

may leave a negative review. But if you ask for a review the right way, you'll be pleased with the results.

How to Get Good Reviews

When it comes to getting good reviews from your customers, you must begin by delivering a consistent and positive user experience. Focusing on the user experience is the best ally for preventing negative reviews from happening. Do you have a process to greet your customers? Do you have a process to help them quickly get the product or service they are seeking to purchase? What type of follow up do you do to assess their satisfaction? Are you able to identify which clients are unhappy? What are you doing to make sure you're exceeding expectations for the majority of your customers? Think about ways to get a pulse on what's happening before someone takes their case to the web, social media, or email.

If you're not already delivering a consistent, positive experience to your customers, then you know where you need to start. Asking an employee to say, "Is there anything else I can help you with?" at the end of a transaction is not only essential, but expected. Asking, "On a scale of 1 to 10 how would your rate the service your received? What could we have done to make it a ten?" is even better. I personally know many small business owners who take a lax

approach to the customer purchase cycle. They are the ones who find themselves dealing with negative reviews. At the same time I see plenty of businesses receiving positive reviews, tons of referrals, and a growing business day after day.

I'm sure you've heard about the surveys that say happy customers tell an average of ten other people about their experience. It's true. Focusing on customer experience isn't just a good idea, it's imperative to the success of your business both online and offline.

Once you've nailed down your in-store, web-based, and phone customer experience(s), try the following for soliciting positive reviews.

1) Ask the Right Customers for Reviews

This may see pretty straight forward, but the best way to get a positive review is to ask the right customers. If you don't ask, you won't receive. But this suggestion goes beyond the surface. Don't ask just any customer to write a review, ask your best customers.

I'm sure you have long-time customers, new customers, repeat purchasers and people you've developed personal relationships with over time. These are the customers you should be asking for

reviews. Simply put, if you want positive reviews, ask the right people.

There are a number of ways to find customers who are getting the most value out of your products and services. Focus on those who are *referring* others to your business, *purchase frequently* (or high ticket items), and those who have been with you for a *long-time*. Ask them to visit Google, Yelp, or another review site and share their experience. Don't aks them for a "positive" review. Doing so is a bit presumptive and a little inappropriate. If you're asking the right person, you don't have to worry about what they're writing.

2) Ask For Reviews at the Right Time

The best time to ask for a review is immediately after you've delivered a great service or someone has purchased a product. Unfortunately, many business owners don't ask for a review and if they do, its days or weeks later. I'm sure this has happened to you. Week's after you've purchased an item you get an email asking for feedback and you can't even remember what you bought!

When you delay the "ask", you force your patrons to do the hard work of remembering the details of their purchase and risk having

them either forget about the experience or worse yet, misinterpret the experience they had.

The best time to ask for a review is when the value you've delivered to the customer is fresh on their mind, making it easy to recall the details of their experience. This increases the likelihood of leaving a positive and detailed review. Your goal should be to ask your customers about their experience within 24 – 48 hours after they buy from you.

In addition to sending follow up emails or making calls within a day or two of their interaction with you, consider asking for reviews when patrons hit a key anniversary, send you positive feedback via email, write a thank you note, or answer favorably to a customer survey.

3) Ask For Reviews In the Right Way

The last thing you want to do is explicitly ask your customers to submit only positive reviews.

Making such a request can come across as "cheap" and can negatively impact your reputation.

There are plenty of ways to ask for favorable reviews but simply coming right out and saying, "Please give us a 5-star review" seldom works. One of the best approaches is to reframe the 'Ask' is to say something like, "If you've had a positive experience, we'd love for you to share it with others (click here to leave review). If not, we want to make it right. Please call us immediately at (555) 123-4567."

While you should be asking for reviews never ask for just a good review. Instead, ask for an honest review. I've seen a number of car dealers do this well, "In a day you'll receive a phone call asking how we did, if you had a positive experience we'd appreciate a 5-star rating, if not, here's my manager's card. Please call him and let us know how we can make your experience better. We're always striving to improve our service."

When you begin asking for reviews the right way, you can quickly begin accumulating positive content on the web about your business. This has a direct and positive impact on your local listings and search engine results. Whether you want it to happen or not, people are already talking about your business online.

What happens if you get a bad review?

Negative reviews are inevitable. However, bad reviews are also an opportunity to learn how to improve your business and make a lasting impression online. DON'T IGNORE NEGATIVE REVIEWS. The best things you can do after you receive a negative online review is to calmly and politely respond to the negative review online. Something like the following would be appropriate, *"Mr. Client, we apologize that your experience was less than exceptional. Our goal is to make sure every customer receives strong value from our services. Please call us at 1-800-123-4567 so we can help you personally."* This type of response helps your business establish trust and credibility with customers you ask to provide reviews and those researching your business online. An additional benefit is that you'll see the average sentiment of your reviews improve and customers will see the value of working with your brand.

Won't everyone ask for their money back? This is a question I often get and the answer is NO. I've worked with thousands of companies over the past 15 years and it simply isn't the case. Your real customers won't change who they are based on a review they saw about someone else's personal situation. Your customers are good people and they understand that you simply can't make everyone

happy. If you're not comfortable putting details of a customer interaction onine, omit it. The most important thing to take-a-way is that the fear of mass refunds simply isn't justified.

Here's a great email template for soliciting positive reviews

I recommend sending the following email to customers immediately after they've left your store or the evening after they made a purchase. It's all about who you ask and the timing of the ask.

Hello [firstname]

I just noticed that you (visited our store, achieved a milestone, or received a service). We are thrilled that you're getting value from (name of your company) and appreciate your business.

If it's not too much trouble, I have a quick request. Could you please leave an honest review on (Google My Business, Yelp, TripAdvisor, etc...)? Here's a link.

Even a sentence or two would be hugely appreciated. If your review helps us get more awesome customers like you, we'll be able to continue delivering the (products/services) you've come to value.

Thanks, and if there's anything at all that we can do to help you in the future, don't hesitate to let me know.

Sincerely,
Your Name, Title

P.S. We love our customers. If there's something we can do to improve our service please call me directly at (555) 123-4567.

4) If You Don't Get a Response Keep Asking.

If you send an email follow up to your customers asking for a review, and don't get a response, ask again. Using third-party software, you can send multiple reminders to clients. Alternatively, you can send a second or third email to those who did not open the first. Personally I believe that asking once or twice is okay, more than that and you could upset your customer. People who are willing to leave a positive review will usually do so on the first or second touch.

5) Respond to All Online Reviews Positive and Negative

Most businesses I work with only focus on responding to negative reviews, but people are tickled pink when you respond to a positive review as well. This shows your level of engagement wich customers and true appreciation for their loyalty. Responding to a positive review reinforces their value and your appreciation for their business. Try to respond to both positive and negative reviews on a regular basis.

Using Reviews to Your Advantage

Positive reviews don't just happen by themselves. They happen when you provide great customer journeys and have a process for requesting reviews from your best customers.

By treating your customers' the best way you know how, you can increase the chances of having them share positive stories online and tell others about their experiences. Positive online reviews are within your reach when you ask for them.

Lesson 7: Website Development

When marketing your local business online you have to start with a good looking mobile responsive website that works for you 24/7. What most business owners don't understand is that developing a high functioning website, one that captures leads and promotes your brand in an optimized way, is now easier than ever before.

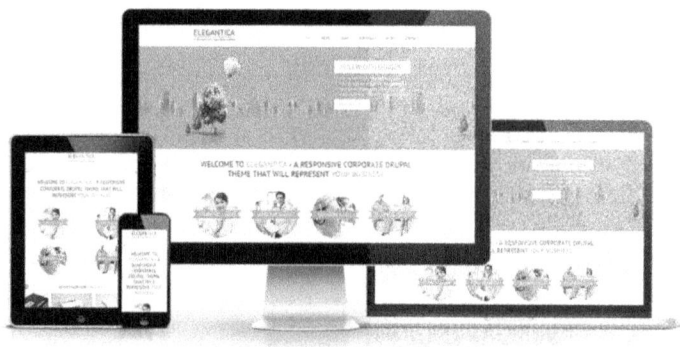

There are a number of solutions available today for launching or updating your website that were previously unavailable. In this section I'll explain all of your options for updating an existing website with a new look and feel, optimizing it in local search results, and how to launch a brand new site quickly and affordably if starting from scratch.

The best place to begin any web development effort (or redevelopment) is with a responsive WordPress Theme for Local Marketing. "Responsive" means your website can be viewed on absolutely any device of any size. The technology recognizes the type of device someone is viewing your site on and reformats its automatically to fit their screen and provide a seamless navigation experience.

Responsive WordPress themes are the future made present for extraordinary local business websites. With a WordPress Theme you can do almost anything you want with your website just by installing a plug-in. This includes event scheduling, adding pictures of your store, or providing social sharing buttons.

There are some really great places to find nice looking Local Marketing WordPress Themes, ready to be installed, customized and applied to your website. Later in this program, I'll show you how to

find an inexpensive resource to help you make the changes to your website for you. In the meantime, let me explain the process of updating your website:

1) Purchase a hosting account and tranfer your domain. I strongly recommend Godaddy.com which makes this easy to do and has great support!

2) Work with your hosting provider to install the WordPress Application.

3) Purchase and install a mobile responsive website template or downloaded one from WordPress.

4) Update your site with your business information.

I know it's a bit of an oversimplification, but that's it! Today, the process of creating and designing your website is pretty straightforward. *See my video where I take you through a live example of revising an existing website using WordPress and a mobile responsive template.* The point I'm trying to make is this – if you don't like your existing website, you can build a new one and it doesn't cost more than a couple of hundred bucks. More importantly, new templates allow for local search engine optimization giving you a greater presence on the web.

To find a mobile responsive template, Google "Local Marketing WordPress Theme" and you'll find a ton of great templates to use. Alternatively you can visit Word Press sites that sell different themes.

Themeforest.net is one of the greatest places to find some really nice responsive WordPress themes especially for your local business. You just search for what you need and you'll find multiple options.

InkThemes.com has an extraordinary collection of local WordPress themes as well. They will even show you some live examples of the different Themes and by resizing your browser allowing you to check different formats and see how responsive the theme actually is.

TemplateMonster.com is a very large source of templates and offers some pretty competitive rates. We've been using them for years to help customers seeking a new, responsive web design.

WordPress.org gives you a lot free WordPress themes, but not many are focused on professional templates. Wordpress will give you access to free theme samples for testing purposes but may be general in nature requiring a bit more customization.

You can also visit other websites listed on Google to find some awesome ideas and many more free business theme samples to try out.

Digital Assets

One of the most important things you can do to fully optimize your website, local listings, and social media is to develop digital assets to be used on and off your website. What are digital assets? A digital asset is any content you develop that is not in text form: images, video, power points, pdf documents, sound clips, etc.

Google favors different types of content. The more diverse your content, the more authority your website can achieve – improving rankings on local search results. When you create digital assets, distribute them through social media and other channels to help spread the word among your target audience. Here are some things to consider:

Video. Create video testimonials and post them on your site and Youtube. Youtube videos do great in search engine results and can drive more traffic to your website. Interview people in your store or ask customers to provide a video testimonial.

Images. People are largely visual. As the famous proverb says, "A picture is worth a thousand words." Additionally, images show in search results, can be used for social media, and improve engagement. Take pictures of the outside of your store, inside of your store, staff, customers, and products to post to the web.

Power Point. Giving a lecture or local presentation? Brand your Powerpoint and upload to Slideshare or similar service. A power point deck will provide additional exposure and points of entry.

PDF's. Have a flyer, sell sheet, or tip sheet? Save it as a PDF and post to your website. Always use a keyword as your file name and provide a title relevant to your business. Search engines will crawl this document and return a listing in search results. As a best practice, include your website URL in the footer of all PDF documents.

Sound Clips. If you are doing interviews or collecting testimonials, always take a sound clip with you. In addition to using it on your website to improve engagement and exposure, you may consider using sound clips as a way to solicit additional interviews by local radio stations. Always write an optimized description on your site that describes your sound clip.

As you can see, there's plenty of help for you to create a really nice professional local business website and digital assets to make your business stand out. You can find plenty of videos on YouTube and even WordPress theme vendors who have their own training on how to install WordPress and website themes. Our video training program covers this topic in further detail but the essential take-away is that you need a website that is mobile responsive and serves as the foundation for a good customer experience. Begin with a good hosting company like Godaddy and be sure to build your site on a platform like Wordpress. Websites should not only look good and create a positive user experience they should also be optimized for search engines. In the next section, I'll cover some of the basics for having a well optimized site that will show up in local search results.

Lesson 8: Website Optimization

If you have an existing website, there are a variety of techniques you can use to optimize the site for appearing in local search results. When someone is searching for a local solution to their need or problem you want your site to appear in organic search results as

well as local listings (aka "Google My Business"). Here are a few tips you can use to implement or share with your webmaster , increasing exposure for your website.

In my best-selling book, SEO Made Simple, I give all the insider secrets you need for achieving a number one Google ranking for your business. But before you go down the rabbit hole, make sure you have the basics covered. Top rankings are based on fundamentals first and foremost.

Here are a few things to consider for local optimization:

1. **Include contact information.** Google is constantly looking to verify your business information. One way they do so is by crawling your website and looking for basic business information such as name and address. I'm still amazed by the number of local practitioners who don't include their address and phone number on the home page or footer of their website. Don't make prospects or Google search for your basic business information.

2. **Contact Us Page.** In addition to including your address and phone in the footer of your website, make sure it appears on every page, have a clean and informative "Contact" page that includes a Google Map, address, phone number, and inquiry

form. Always make sure the address matches exactly what you have on the footer and home page of your site.

3. **About Us Page.** The about us page is one of the most popular pages of any website. Include pictures, video, and/or text describing your business and what makes you unique.   This page will show up in search results so be sure to give prospective customers a reason to vist your store.

4. **Service Areas.** If you draw from a specific area such as local cities, list them somewhere on your website. You can include individual web pages customized to each area or simply a listing of the cities you serve. This targets individuals who are searching for your product or service in a specific area. For example, they may use a query such as "Dry Cleaner in Hamilton, NJ". If your listing information includes the Hamilton, NJ service area, it will help Google prioritize your webpage over someone elses. Combined with local search, this will help improve local online presence.

Optimizing your website for local search doesn't have to be complicated. If you apply the basic techniques above, making sure to learn simple on-page strategies like using meta data, titles, image tags, etc., you can quickly improve organic results. Many people are overwhelmed by the concept of search engine optimization but it's

actually much easier than you might think. Learn more here or by downloading, SEO Made Simple (5th Edition).

Mobile Optimization

The whole world is surfing the web on mobile devices. According to experts on the subject, it has been discovered that if you don't have a mobile strategy you can't connect with over half of your audience! People check their mobile devices dozens of times a day, so it makes good sense to get your business in on the non-stop action by going mobile.

Do you realize how important Mobile Marketing is at this very moment?

The number of mobile devices almost exceeds the number of people on earth. As a result, you have to optimize your website and other digital assets for mobile viewing.

- ✓ One in three online searches is done on a mobile device
- ✓ The average American spends 2 hours a day on his or her mobile device
- ✓ 68% of people use a mobile device to look up a store address

- ✓ 52% of mobile users check the prices of an item online they wish to buy
- ✓ 91% of smart phone users keep their phone within arm's length
- ✓ 70% of all mobile searches result in an action within an hour
- ✓ 52% of mobile searchers call the company they are researching
- ✓ 47% of mobile users are more likely to read reviews online for the product

And did I mention that people are "Googling" their local providers using mobile devices day in and day out?

There are so many ways to optimize your business for mobile. The good news is that most of them are automatic and convenient. The most important is a mobile website.

Mobile Website. If you correctly developed your website on a mobile responsible platform, you have already achieved this extremely important step. A responsive WordPress Website is the best solution for this.

Having a responsive WordPress website will give people the ability to see your local business website from any device. They can visit

your website from a desktop computer or laptop computer or they can check it out on their tablet or mobile phone.

If you've already invested a lot of money on your existing website using a platform that is not mobile responsive, there's a way to create a mobile version of your website so mobile users can visit the mobile version instead of a non-mobile version.

There are essentially two ways to do this: 1) You could create a mobile website from scratch. 2) You can convert your existing website into a mobile website.

There are a number of solutions that help you create or modify existing sites to make them moble responsive. JQMBuilder.com offers an absolutely simple and effective platform to create your mobile website in a matter of minutes. JQMBuilder is a powerful onlIne tool that can produce basic professional looking jQucry Mobile Websites in minutes. They will train you step by step how to do it by yourself.

Regardless of what platform you choose, having a mobile optimized site is paramount. Google provides a tool to check the mobile responsiveness of your website which is available for free at https://www.google.com/webmasters/tools/mobile-friendly/

If you use the tool and discover that your site is not mobile responsive, use the resources noted above or upgrade your site to a mobile responsive platform.

We'll discuss other forms of local mobile marketing later in this guide. The of this section has been to address your website optimization needs and help you realize that it's essential to design for mobile (this includes your website, digital assets, email, etc.).

Lesson 9: Google Analytics

Google Analytics is a great way to learn more about your website traffic and therefore the audience interested in your products and services. Google Analytics, also referred to as "G" "A", is a web analytics service offered by Google that tracks and reports website activity, audience, and traffic sources. Google launched the service over a decade ago and has been improving functionality ever since. Google Analytics is now the most widely used web analytics platform in the world.

Here are a few basic things Google Analytics can measure if added to your website which can be done by adding a small piece of code in your website footer. If using WordPress, you can install a plugin

that will add Google Analytics code for you, providing immediate access to traffic and other data including:

Sessions. A session is a group of interactions a user takes within a given time frame while on your website. Google Analytics defaults the time frame to 30 minutes.

Users. This refers to the number of distinct individuals requesting pages from the website during a given period, regardless of how often they visit.

Pageviews. This counts all the times the page was viewed in an individual session as a single event. If a visitor viewed the page once in their visit or five times, the number of unique pageviews will be recorded as just one.

New vs. Returning Visitors. New visitors are individuals who have not visited your site before during a specific time period. Returning visitors will have previously made at least one visit to one page on your site. This is determined based on a variety of factors including whether or not Google can detect cookies, indicating previous visits. If Google cannot detect a website cookie, one will be set for future tracking unless the user has disabled cookies in their personal browser preferences.

Segments. Segments enable you to analyze your data in more detail by filtering the results to show information for certain kinds of traffic. You can also use segments to compare results between groups of visitors (example: new vs. returning, or paid vs. organic search traffic).

Bounce Rate. Bounce rate is given as a percentage, and represents the number of visits when users leave your site after just one page regardless of how they got to your site or how long they stayed on that page. A home page bounce rate of about 50% is pretty common.

Visitors Flow. This analytics feature shows you how users moved throughout your website from landing page to exit page. Visitors flow reports can be customised to show additional details such as the geographic location of users or the traffic source. Visitor flow also shows how many people exited at each stage of the interaction.

Traffic Sources: Direct vs. Referral. Traffic sources show you how users got to your site, and in Google Analytics are split into direct and referral traffic.

Direct traffic is made up of visitors that type a URL directly into the address bar, select an auto-complete option when typing the URL, or click on a bookmark to get to your site.

Referral traffic is when a user has landed on your site by clicking on a link from somewhere else. This may be another website, a social media post, or a search engine.

Search Traffic: Organic vs. Paid. Google Analytics lets you see what percentage of your traffic came from search engines. This data is then broken down further to indicate organic and paid search.

Organic search shows users who came to your site by clicking on the organic links on the search engine results page. These results appear below paid ads, often indicated with an "Ad" notification and determined by how well the page is optimized for search engines.

The paid search results show users who clicked on one of your paid search engine ads. These ads appear at the top or bottom of search engine results pages and are managed via Google AdWords.

Google Analytics is the best way to understand your online audience, how you acquired them, and their behavior. With this information, you're better armed to customize your website, online marketing, and communications to prospects and customers. Don't

Page 48

underestimate the value of good data and be sure to install Google Analytics on your website. If you don't know how to do so, use a freelancer who can install the code properly. This information will give you a significant advantage over your competition because it provides insights into who is showing interest in your product and services.

Lesson 10: Google Webmaster Tools

In additiona to great tools to measure website traffic, Google also provides a tool that tells you how to improve your wesbite to show up in more Google search results. A lot of people don't even know this tool exists but it's worth it's weight in gold.

Google Webmaster Tools is one of the most valuable resources you can use for identifying the best way to optimize your website. This is Google's very own resource for identifying things you can change on your website, directions on how to improve website accessibility, as well as strategies for increasing organic rankings.

Why would Google provide such a tool? The reason is because Google is interested in creating the best user experience posible – that's why people keep coming back to Google and using it time and

again. If you apply all of their optimization suggestions, users are going to have a good experience when clicking through to your site.

The easiest way to get started with Google Webmaster tools is by registering online for this free tool. You sync up your website with Google Webmaster Tools through a simple verification process. There are multiple options you can choose from, making it really easy to claim a particular site you own. Once you verify your listing, Google Webmaster Tools will give you access to a customized dashboard.

Your dashboard will show you everything you need at a glance. Features such as "Crawl Errors" will show you what needs to be fixed on your site to better optimize your website pages.

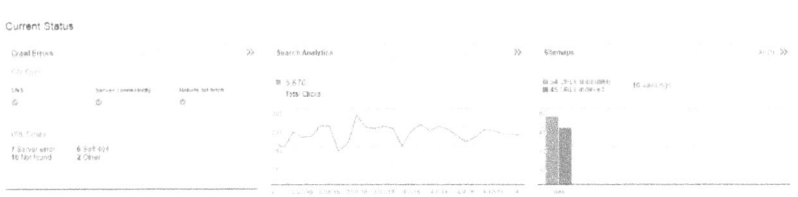

Another option that I have found valuable is under "Search Appearance". Click on the "HTML improvements menu item and you'll see Google's interpretation of what on your site needs a little

work. Whether it's adding a meta title or description, using Google's suggestions are vital for optimizing your online exposure.

One of the most important things you can use Google Webmaster Tools for is uploading a sitemap. Submitting a sitemap is a great way to inform Google that you're actively managing your website. To simplify the process and generate a sitemap for free, go to xml-sitemaps.com. All you have to do is enter your URL and the tool creates an xml and .html sitemap for you. The .html sitemap should be added to your website (if using WordPress, just use a plugin). If you're not using Wordpress you'll need to host the sitemap on your hosting account. If you don't know how to do so, use a freelander to do this work for you.

More importantly, the .xml sitemap should be upload to Google Webmaster Tools. Click on the Crawl > Sitemaps tab and click "Add/Test Sitemap". Once you've uploaded the sitemap, Google will verify it and show you the status in your dashboard. By leveraging the information that Google is providing, you can give your website better rankings and start to control more online real estate – driving potential buyers to your local business.

Lesson 11: Content Marketing (Blogging)

Everywhere you turn people are talking about content marketing but the truth is that content marketing is nothing new. Anyone who does online marketing knows that information gets stale if you don't make frequent updates. As a result, you have to continually update the information you publish as well as content for social media channels in order to keep things relevant and timely. Keeping things updated benefits online interactions and also helps improve organic search results. To take the mystery out of content marketing, I want you to focus on one thing – Blogging. The concept of blogging is simple and helps you to build a brand online, expand the size of your website, and generate more leads and traffic organically.

What is blogging?

The concept of blogging has been around forever (if you'd like an in-depth review of blogging, be sure to check out my top-selling book, "Blogging Made Simple" on Amazon.com). The general principle is that you publish content, usually in the form of an article, and enhance the content with either images or video, that covers a specific topic. Some bloggers are 'experts' in a given area and publish content related to their field, others publish 'how to'

content about their area of expertise. Some blogs are focused on a particular topic, often referred to as a niche, but some content is sourced through interviews or guests who have deep knowledge about a specific area. I find my business clients always have expertise in something and can generally write a number of articles covering their area of focus. For example, someone who has a bait and tackle shop can write blog articles all year-round about the fish that are in season, the type of bait to use, and the area's best fishing spots. Professionals like accountants can talk about new accounting pricinciples, how to manage your financies, and how to prepare for taxes. The idea is simple, share your expertise through articles that are enhanced with images, video, and other digital assets to build your brand online.

Blog about what you know

There is tremendous value in blogging for your business. When you provide content about your area of expertise, it positions you and your business as the go-to resource in the area. Additionally, you are providing useful content to prospects and customers who will feel a need to reciprocate if regularly consuming your information. And lastly, having new content published on a regular basis is like putting your website on steroids. Search engines like Google love

original content and give you extra points when they see people interacting with new content and then sharing that content through social media and other channels.

Here are a few tips to consider, making content work as part of your local marketing strategy.

- Create a content calendar that features what topics you'll cover during different months of the year
- Add a blog to your website if haven't already done so. Ask a freelancer to help if you don't know how.
- Inform local media of your blog. Give them permission to reprint the content as long as they give you/your business credit and point to you on the web
- Make your blog posts around 500 words and include images or video with each post. Longer posts are better
- Make it easy for individuals to share your post on social media and other channels (you can use a plugin or Sharethis button)
- Create content on a regular Schedule. This is not a set and forget strategy. Produce 1 – 4 articles per month
- Promote your blog posts on your social media accounts immediately after publishing.

Content marketing doesn't have to be a chore. There are plenty of sources you can use for getting your blog set up, producing and promoting content. Again, Wordpress is a good platform for blogging but any website should be able to accommodate the addition of new content on a regular basis.

I encourage you to begin with a content marketing calendar. Write out on a sheet of paper what topics you'll cover in the weeks and months to come. Sit down and start writing one post per week, add it to your website, and put a link to the content in your next Facebook post. Don't try to over complicate this thing called 'content marketing'. The goal is to produce thematic content that shows your expertise and helps your business grow. As you being adding content to your site, you'll see customer engagement grow, improved organic rankings, and more activity online that helps promote your brand.

Lesson 12: Lead Capture

So far we've discussed local directories, your website, the creation of online digital assets, and content development. But what's the goal? It's all about getting in front of prospective customers and turning them into paying customers. This is where Lead Capture

comes into play and its one of the most important topics we'll cover in this guide. Lead capture is essential for dominating the local online landscape and growing your business. Let's begin by explaining the role of lead capture, describing how it works, and then exploring simple ways to implement lead capture functionality.

The Power of Online Lead Generation

After attracting people to your website, what's the next step? Depending on your business, you may be looking for prospects to raise their hand and show their interest, schedule an appointment, or make an online purchase. These actions should be measurable and meaningful. The question to ask yourself is, "How can I help my potential customer get the information they need in the most efficient and effective way possible? Once they get the information they need, what's the next step?"

I've spent full consulting days with businesses helping them answer some of these fundamental questions – but the answers are usually the same. Local businesses want someone to visit their website and either complete an inquiry form, make a phone call, or visit the store.

For these individuals it comes down to prioritizing information on your website. Is your address featured prominently on your home page? Your address? Your hours of operation? If not, you should make those changes immediately. Use your Google My Business profile to gain insight into the type of information people want to see. From your address to photos of your business, Google knows what people are looking for and thanks to Google Analytics and other reporting you should know as well.

Although you have a number of people who visit your site for specific information, you also have a second group which consists of people are browsing. This group is usually research options and comparing possible providers but not ready ot make a purchase.

Looking but not ready to buy

What should you do with website visitors who are considering your business but aren't quite ready to buy? This is where lead capture becomes so important and the most powerful word in marketing comes in to play, "FREE". The best way to lure prospective customers into becoming paying customers is through what's called a drip campaign.

Although this concept of a drip campaign has evolved over time, the premise is pretty straight forward. You simply offer a website visitor or prospect something for free in exchange for a name and or email address. Capturing this information allows you to have an ongoing dialog with them, dripping valuable content on a regular basis – keeping your brand in front of them and providing additional incentives to buy from you. Your business may also decide to implement a remarketing campaign, using a service like Google Adwords remarketing, to show prospective customers ads after they leave your website and start looking elsewhere. Now, lets talk about how drip campaigns are created and how to structure a campaign for optimal conversions.

A drip campaign is developed using an auto responder. The concept behind an autoresponder is pretty simple. You develop a series of emails that a prospect will receive (automatically) after they provide an email address. For example, if you offer a free resource on your website such as a list of, "Top 10 things to consider before buying a used car", your prospective customer would be required to enter an email address to gain access to the article or document. Once an email is provided, the tool, called an autoresponder, would automatically send an email to this individual with a link to the download. A day or two later it might send another email talking

about the best used cars to purchase and then two day after that send another email talking about the best way to finance a used car. Two days after that, another email talking about the most reliable used cars. And so on, and so on. Some email autoresponders provide a year worth of emails, others provide just a few touches. The goal is to move prospects along the purchase decision process and autoresponders are a great way to do so without employing sales people.

Example of an auto-responder sequence (Aweber):

1	Your Download Link for 15 Ways to Prot... Send a test · Delete · Copy to Drafts · Settings	Send immediately	0 spam score	21 opens
2	Hope is NOT a strategy! Send a test · Delete · Copy to Drafts · Settings	Sent 3 days after the previous message	0 spam score	45 opens
3	You Are Not Going to Believe This! Send a test · Delete · Copy to Drafts · Settings	Send 3 days after the previous message	0 spam score	30 opens
4	The 3 Most Common Questions People ... Send a test · Delete · Copy to Drafts · Settings	Send 2 days after the previous message	0 spam score	4 opens
5	This Company Increased Revenue 32%... Send a test · Delete · Copy to Drafts · Settings	Send 3 days after the previous message	0 spam score	12 opens
6	Questions You Should Be Asking Send a test · Delete · Copy to Drafts · Settings	Send 3 days after the previous message	0 spam score	10 opens
7	How To Reach Reputation Nirvana Send a test · Delete · Copy to Drafts · Settings	Send 3 days after the previous message	0 spam score	16 opens

There are a number of email providers that allow you to set up a series of emails to fire automatically once an action is taken. Essentially, when someone provides you with an email, it triggers a series of messages or touches. Messages are created in advance and

then triggered automatically after an individual has provided an email address. Mailchimp, Constant Contact, Aweber, etc. are all affordable resources you can use to set up autoresponders on your website.

Attract Bees With Honey

There are a number of ways to get prospects into your marketing funnel. As I mentioned above, giving them something for free is always the place to start. The question I seem to get a lot is what to offer. Personally, I prefer to give prospects a free Resource Guide. When you can provide valuable resources at no cost, people take interest. The guide obviously needs to be related to your business so think about what might be most helpful to those in your niche. Creating this resource is easy, simply create a list of resources you use with a small description for each and save it as a PDF. This document can be hosted online and your first email, after someone has logged in, can provide a link to the document. Alternatively, you could provide access to a special video you've created with tips, strategies, or a product review. The options are limitless. Personally, I like to test a bunch of different options and see which free resource creates the most interest among prospects.

I strongly encourage you to add an autoresponder to your website. This is the best way I know to get those who are interested, but not ready to buy, into your marketing funnel. When they are ready to purchase it's your brand, your products and services, that will be in front of them thanks to the emails you've been sending. Consider informing your list of any specials you are offering as well. Sometime it takes a small incentive to get people to try your products or services the first time.

CAN-SPAM

As a professional marketer I'm obligated to tell you about email marketing law. You are NOT allowed to illegally acquire or scrape personal email addresses from the web. In fact, you shouldn't be using an email address unless someone has provided a double opt-in, explicitly requesting to be added to your list. That being said if someone provides you their email through an opt-in, located on your website, you have a right to market to them.

Using an autoresponder is also a great way to manage your email list. Each email provider handles 'unsubscribes' on your behalf, giving individuals an opportunity to remove themselves from your list and avoiding future emails. If you had to do this manually, it would be a chore and difficult to manage. Don't try to manage your

email list on your own, find an auto-responder and determine what offer you are going to test.

The next step is draft a series of emails that provide valuable content for your list. Write something on your own or find a freelancer who can create this for you. The next step is to launch the autoresponder by placing an opt-in box on your website. The major services all have WordPress plugins you can use or you can simply hire a freelander to implement this basic functionality on your site. As your list grows, you'll have more and more prospectics in your pipeline that over time will begin to convert and help you grow your business thanks to your autoresponder.

Some marketing funnels can be very intricate and complex when using autoresponders. If you're just starting out, keep it simple. Using a resource like we mentioned above (ex: Aweber) that allows a form to be placed on your website and an auto responder to provide content until prospective customers are ready to buy (some of the content should include discounts or promotions) is the best and most effective way to get started.

The goal is to get people interested in your services and make it really easy for them to do business with you.

Lesson 13: Facebook

Social Media giant Facebook has invested a great deal of money, time, and effort into positioning local businesses on their proprietary advertising platform. This is because most people spend their time browsing social media to connect with friends, both local and far away, search for something new, share experiences or listen to conversations. And many of those conversations have to do with local businesses.

How many times have you seen your friends post selfies from a local restaurant or take a snap shot of their experience at a local venue, showing off their night out on the town? Due to the nature of social media, it has become a great way to not only share new things about you and your business but also to target people in your local community. With the advent of a highly sophisticated, yet simple to use targeting option, Facebook is the best place to start promoting your business on social media.

Additionally, I have found amazing results for local clients simply using Facebook ads targeted to a specific geographic area. Your target market is likely on Facebook throughout the day. Are they seeing your business or your competitor?

Facebook Page

Getting your business listed on Facebook couldn't be easier. The best place to start is with your own Facebook account. Begin by clicking on the drop down option in the upper right-hand corner of your screen.

When you use the drop down, you will see an option that says, "Create a Page". This page gives you simple options for getting started. Are you a local business? If so, click on the "Local Business or Place" icon and Facebook will walk you through the Facebook Page setup.

As of this writing, Facebook has simplified the process by getting you started with just basic business information such as name, address and phone. Be sure to fill in these options and click on the "Get Started" button.

I encourage you to continue and complete all of the additional information requested. Facebook pages benefit from lots of information and resources such as photos - so take the time to enter all of the requested information. This not only helps your company listing stand out, but also gives you a number of ways to effectively manage your Facbeook page. With just some basic information and a few clicks of the mouse, your Business Page is listed on Facebook.

As you can see, Facebook offers a number of settings to help you customize your Facebook page, determine what information appears, and who can access the content. In addition, you can set up others (Page Roles) to help manage your Facebook updates and posting.

LOCAL MARKETING MADE SIMPLE

⚙ **General**	Favorites	Page is not added to Favorites	Edit
💬 Messaging	Page Visibility	Page published	Edit
ⓘ Page Info	Page Verification	Page is not verified	Edit
⋯ Post Attribution	Visitor Posts	Anyone can publish to the Page. Anyone can add photos and videos to the Page	Edit
🔔 Notifications	Audience Optimization for Posts	The ability to select a preferred audience and restrict the audience for your posts is turned off	Edit
👤 Page Roles	Messages	People can contact my Page privately	Edit
People and Other Pages	Tagging Ability	Only people who help manage my Page can tag photos posted on it	Edit
📱 Apps	Others Tagging this Page	People and other Pages can tag my Page	Edit
📷 Instagram Ads	Country Restrictions	Page is visible to everyone	Edit
⭐ Featured	Age Restrictions	Page is shown to everyone	Edit
🎧 Page Support	Page Moderation	No words are being blocked from the Page	Edit
	Profanity Filter	Turned off	Edit
≣ Activity Log	Similar Page Suggestions	Choose whether your Page is recommended to others	Edit
	Post in Multiple Languages	Ability to write posts in multiple languages is turned off	Edit
	Comment Ranking	Most recent comments are shown for my Page by default	Edit
	Download Page	Download Page	Edit
	Merge Pages	Merge duplicate Pages	Edit
	Remove Page	Delete your Page	Edit

All of this goes a very long way in building an online presence. With the help of Google My Business, Local Search Directory listings, your website, and a Facebook page, you are well on your way to local domination.

Your company Facebook Page works in a similar manner to your personal Facebook account. Schedule daily posts and share information about your business including specials, promotions and other engaging content to get the most from this resource.

As is true with any social account, let your customers know about it. Send an email asking them to follow your page for exciting updates. The greater the following you build, the more people you'll touch in your target area which helps your business stay top of mind and generate referrals. People love to share quality content and special offers via Facebook so always consider how to improve the enagement of your posts.

In addition to creating a Facebook page, there are additional options you can use to start generating more website traffic, local awareness, and most importantly, local leads.

Facebook Advertising

There are over 3 million advertisers on Facebook – and for good reason. Facebook advertising is one of the most effective and affordable ways to promote your local business.

In addition to getting free traffic to your Facebook Page through referrals, search, and other organic means, Facebook also gives you the ability to advertise to as many people as you want within your local area online.

Facebook advertising allows your business to place custom ads or content in front of a specific audience you are trying to reach

through various ad formats and locations. Costs vary based on the reach and engagement an ad receives. Facebook ads can appear in your target audience's News Feed or the right column of Facebook on desktop, as well as News Feed on mobile. Additionally, there are a number of different ad models allowing you to pay for ads based on the number of exposures or each time an ad is clicked on.

When you choose to advertise on Facebook, you're provided with the opportunity to hone in on your audience, which gives you a chance to gain insight about your current and potential customers. The data you collect through Facebook ads then allows you to improve targeting for a more efficient and effective advertising experience. Facebook ads are targeted, flexibile, and a boon to any local business trying to grow their brand and generated customers.

3 Facebook advertising best practices

Before you begin, remember these 3 Facebook advertising best practices:

1. *Always determine your objectives before you start.* It's important to know the purpose of your Facebook ads before you decide on a budget for advertisements. Understand the aim of your compaign. Is it to increase for brand awareness,

conversions, video views, or clicks to your website? Each action made by your audience on your Facebook ad costs money, so be sure to solidify your objectives before making those investments.

2. *Be specific on your audience targeting.* Facebook houses millions, if not billions, of data points. Take the time to get very specific with audience targeting to ensure your ad will appear where people in the target audience will see it.

3. *Rotate your ads regularly.* This is not a set and forget advertising strategy. To avoid ad fatigue, rotate your Facebook ads at least once per month if not weekly. This means that when people start to see your ad too many times, they get bored of it and stop clicking. Unfortunately, when your click-through rate starts to drop, Facebook penalizes you, driving up your cost per click (CPC), making likes, comments, and click-throughs more expensive. This affects both acquisition and engagement campaigns. To avoid this, rotate your ads every 5 - 7 days.

Keeping these tips in mind. Let me get very specific on using Facebook advertising because of its power and the impact I've seen it have on hundreds of businesses. If you're going to take one thing from this guide, it's to learn how to leverage the power of social

media advertising, specifically Facebook, to build your local brand and generate tons of potential customers for your busines.

How to advertise on Facebook

Using these steps that follow, you'll be able to define your objective, target an audience, set a budget, and place your ad. I'll warn you though, once you launch your first campaign and start seeing results, you'll wish you'd been advertising on Facebook long before today.

Step 1: Create a Facebook business page

If you haven't already done so, follow these steps for create your very own Facebook Business page. When creating a Facebook Page, its important to determine the proper category of the Page. Choosing the appropriate category that best describes the nature of your business will help people find your Page more easily and frequently. The category name is displayed on your Page and is one of the first things a user sees when they visit your brand on Facebook.

Go to facebook.com/pages/create

The next step is to choose a page category. Click Get Started and follow the on-screen instructions.

Step 2: Create goals for your Facebook ads

When creating your goals for your Facebook ads, make sure your goals are based on meaningful results. What I mean is that your goals need to be specific, measurable, and attainable. Decide what you want to happen by when. Creating smart goals for your Facebook ads will help you achieve a better return on investment as you begin launching campaigns.

For example, a goal can be, "Acquire 100 registrants for the upcoming Home Improvement Workshop in 2 months." This goal will now guide your Facebook ad strategy and help you choose the right type of Facebook ad, appropriate target, and level of spend.

Step 3: Choose an objective for your campaign

Now that you've created your Facebook Page and have goals for your ads, you can now go into the *Facebook Ad Manager* and choose an objective for your ad. The option I typically choose when working with local businesses is to, **"Reach People Near Your Business"**

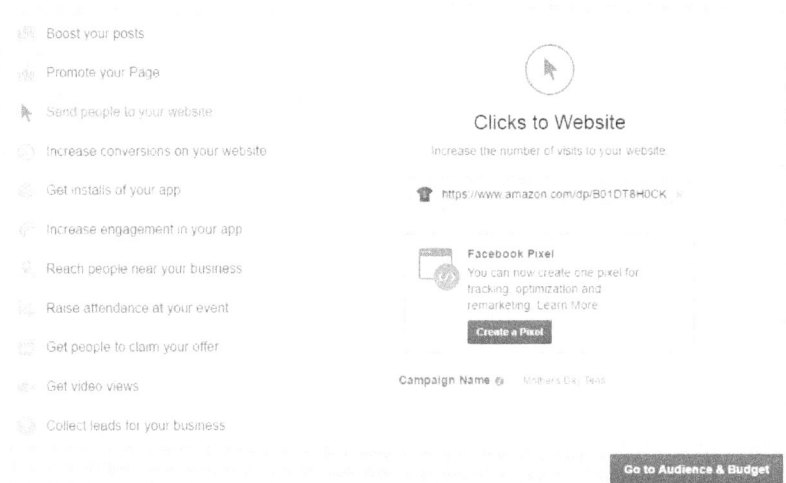

This option is designed for local businesses who want to geo-target the area they serve. I have found this option to be the most effective for local business advertising but have also seen other options being used.

If your goal for example Is to acquire registrants for an upcoming event, the Facebook ad objective you would choose is to "Raise attendance at your event." Or if you want to drive people to your website, then you would choose the objective, "Send people to your website."

Step 4: Choose your target audience and ad spend

This step is crucial in setting your Facebook ad up for success. You can target ads based on location, age, gender, language, interests, and behavior. You can further customize by creating custom audiences to reach people who already know your business, or to remove them from your ad's target audience so you can reach new people on Facebook.

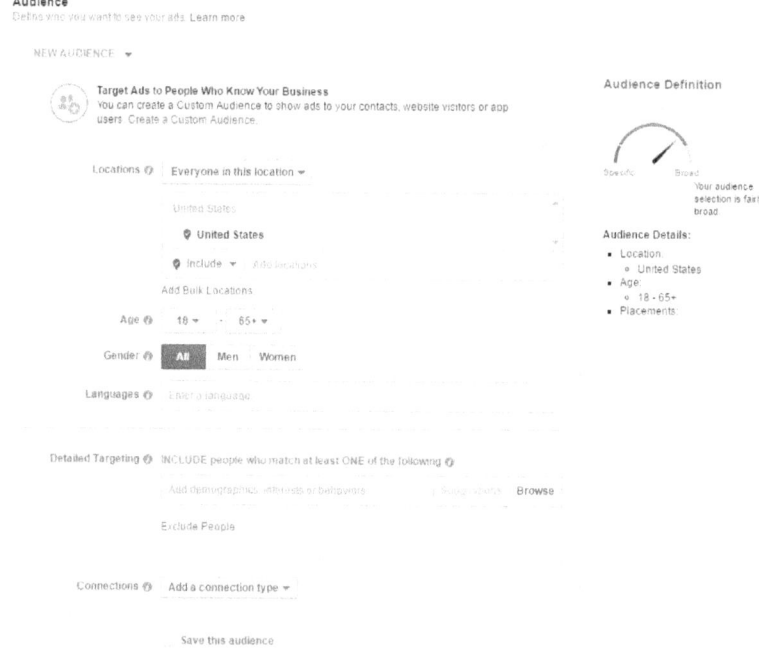

These custom audiences can be created through a customer list, website traffic, or app activity. Facebook is continually adding new features so continue to investigate new targeting activities. You should always be testing new strategies to help you improve conversion rates.

After you're done choosing your target audience, you can then decide how much you want to spend on your ad. Make sure your ad spend is reasonable when starting out. The ad budget you set is the maximum amount you want to spend on a daily basis or for a complete campaign. If you choose to have a daily budget, the amount you enter will be the maximum amount you'll spend each day. Only $5 per day is a great place to start. If you choose a lifetime budget, the amount you enter is the maximum you'll spend during the lifetime of your ad.

Choose to bid for an objective, clicks, or impressions. This will determine how you pay and who your ad will be served to. For example if you optimize for the "Page like" objective, you'll be charged when your ad is shown to people who might be inclined to like your Page. Personally I like the pay-per-click model when available in order to effectively manage expenses and better determine customer acquisition costs.

Choose when you want your ad to run under ad scheduling. If you choose lifetime budget, you choose specific hours and days of the

week for your ad to run. Choosing to run ads on a schedule is the most efficient way to spend your budget. This option allows you to serve your ad when the target audience is most likely engaging on Facebook. For example, if you chose to target a specific location, you want to schedule ads when prospects are awake and active on social media.

Step 5: Choose how you want your ad to look

The actual creation of the ad is the fun part of advertising on Facebook. Choose your images, headline, body text, as well as placement of the actual ad. You can have up to 5 images, and the headline text can only be 25 characters.

What's interesting is that Facebook doesn't want your image to have a lot of copy. They do some type of analysis to determine copy as a percentage of the image. I believe the current threshold is around 20% so look for images that are free of letters and copy. Facebook even gives you access to their library of stock photography for ad creation. Since it is so easy to create good looking Facebook ads, I strongly encourage you to produce the maximum amount of ads to see what will generate the highest conversion.

Keep in mind that because your character limit for a headline is so short, your copy has to be intriguing enough for people to want to click on it. Along with the headline, there is also text that will accompany the post. This can only be 90 characters long, which means your copy needs to effectively and concisely portray what the content is about (think about it as a really good Tweet!).

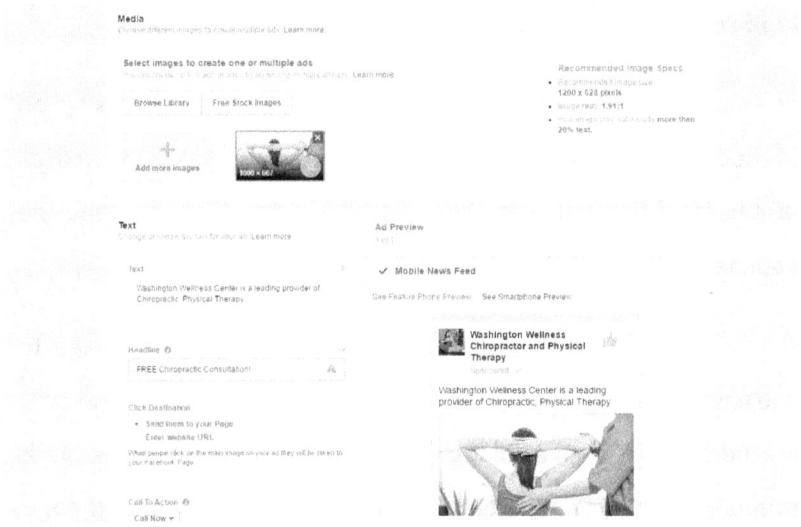

Lastly, you need to choose the placement of your Facebook ad. Choose whether you want the ad to appear on people's desktop news feed, mobile news feed, right column, or audience network.

Step 6: Place your order

Once you're ready for your ad to be reviewed, click on the green button that says Place Order, located on the bottom right-hand corner of your screen. You'll receive an email from Facebook once your ad has been reviewed and approved.

Step 7: Create a Facebook ad report

Now that you have created your Facebook ads, it's important that you report on performance. To create a report on Facebook Ad Manager, click the reports icon in the upper left hand corner of your screen. You can also drill down on any of your campaigns and change the report metrics. You'll automatically see data from the default report called General Metrics over the last 30 days for your active campaigns. As mentioned previously, Facebook is always changing and upgrading their ad system so the best way to evaluate campaigns from my perspective is by clicking into the actual Ad groups themselves and using the data found on the main dashboard. View this data from a variety of perspectives by changing the sorting funcationality using dropdowns provided (ex: Columns: Performance).

Customize the metrics you see in your report and then click the Export button on the top-right column to download your report.

Now that we've covered the basics of Facebook advertising, let's focus on other social channels you can begin using to increase your reach, build your brand, and help dominate local search.

Boost a Post

For people who are a little nervous about online advertising, I completed understand. When I was first introduced to Facebook ads, like anything new, it took me a while to get oriented and understand what I was doing. The good news is that Facebook understands the potential complexity and anxiety some people have in this regard so they created a short cut. What If I told you that with a few clicks of a button, you could easily begin reaching new

potential customers on Facebook for a set daily budget? You'd probably say, "What do you mean and how does it work?"

When a business makes a post or an update to thier timeline, Facebook will automatically give the business an option to "Boost" the post. Essentially, they are saying, "Give us some $ and we'll increase the liklihood that your audience will see your post in their News Feeds." Once you click "Boost Post" you choose the audience and budget you want based on reach and how long you want your boosted campaign to run. When you boost your post, you can target your ad to People who like your Page, People who like your Page and their friends, or People you choose through targeting. If you choose people through the targeting option, you can select location, interests, age and gender.

I've seen some nice results with boosted posts, especially those offering free resources, information, or promotions. If you're looking for simple, but highly effective way to get started with Facebook advertising, I strongly recommend using this option.

Lesson 14: Twitter

Facebook isn't the only social media channel offering online advertising. Twitter also offers some amazing online advertising tools for local businesses that seem similar to Facebook. As with Facebook, Twitter gives your business the option of creating a Twitter Page as well as advertising on their sponsored sections. One of the most important things to know about Twitter however is that recent studies has proven, beyond a shadow of a doubt, that activity on Twitter is directly correlated with improvements in organic search results. Said another way, having a Twitter page is no longer an option but rather an essential part of your local marketing strategy. Begin with a Twitter page that you actively post to on a regular basis.

Twitter Page

Creating a Twitter Page for your business is just as easy as creating a basic twitter account, you just need to use your Local Business details to create the account.

With Twitter you will have a personalized URL identifying your Twitter Page (https://twitter.com/yourcompanyname). This is something that can really boost your brand on the web and should be linked from your website's home page.

Once your page has been developed, consider updating via tweets on a daily basis. You can use helpful tools like Hootsuite, or ask someone in your office to post and repost content on a regular basis. If you're not familiar with how to make the most of Twitter, watch a few YouTube videos or hire a freelancer to develop posts.

Advertising on Twitter

Twitter is the place that many people go to discover what's happening right now. Twitter ads are designed to help you connect with this just-in-time audience and get results that drive action and add value. For those businesses seeking to build an audience, website traffic, generate sales, promote an app, or simply create brand awareness, Twitter is a powerful option.

For certain local businesses, Twitter can be a great online marketing channel. Twitter is particularly effective for local restaurants and retailers that are more inclined to generate check-ins and posts from in-store customers. Local marketers can and should capitalize on this organic traffic by using Twitter as a vehicle to promote special offers, discounts, and product/menu updates that drive consumers to their locations and entice them to spend and spend some more.

Service-based businesses such as real estate, plumbers and landscapers who are more focused on lead generation should be using Twitter to supplement their efforts rather than use it as a main lead source. These businesses do not typically benefit from posting and/or promoting constant updates on Twitter.

A better way to use Twitter is to increase mind share among prospects and customers. You can do this by tweeting out a link to your latest blog post, customer testimonial, online newsletter or updated business information. These types of announcements can increase awareness of your services and help create a unique personality for your business.

Beyond posting updates, Twitter offers businesses a variety of local advertising options, such as:

Promoted Tweets

Promoted tweets are regular tweets that target current and potential followers. These ad-driven posts help local businesses engage with new prospects. When thinking about the concept of a promoted tweet, think about a boosted post. They are pretty much the same thing. As mentioned earlier, if you're going to boost or highlight a post, you want it to provide some type of incentive. Experiment with different options and see which ones provide the greatest engagement.

Promoted Accounts

In addition to the promoted tweet, businesses can create a promoted account to generate new followers. For example, local businesses often benefit from promoting their account during a seasonal campaign. The thought process here is that by adding more people into your follower list, you can increase total engagement. Twitter will display your business profile to users in the "Who to follow" section. Using this option, you only pay when a new follwer is added. There was a time when adding followers cost pennies but unfortunately this option has gotten more expensive. None-the-less, if you are actively managing your Twitter account, each new

follower can become a qualified prospect, so experiment with the promoted accounts option.

Promoted Trends

Twitter also offers promoted trends, which are placed next to a user's Twitter timeline. Targeting promoted trends to specific geographies helps capture prospects' attention at the local level. This can be powerful for franchise trying to reach more customers at a local level. In addition to trends, businesses can also use ZIP code targeting for promoting tweets and accounts.

Advertising Alternatives

If you're not sold on the idea of Twitter Advertising, that's okay. Just like Facebook, there's an easier option for local businesses. One way to grow your Twitter following without spending money on ads is to begin posting regularly using hashtags like #keepitlocal or #hamiltonlocal. Contact your township or chamber of commerce to see what hashtags they use to promote local businesses. This can go a very long way in growing your following and help you to get the most from Twitter.

As with any form of social media advertising, its essential to monitor your ad spend and results. It's the only way to know if your

marketing dollars are working to your benefit. Also, focus on free social media promotion (posting regularly, hashtags, etc.) before going down the path of paid advertising.

What we've seen so far with Twitter is that ads have been most effective for large retail and restaurant brands. However, it always pays to try new forms of marketing and social media advertising. You may find something that works for you at an extremely low cost.

Lesson 15: Adwords

There are entire courses focused on Google Adwords and even an official Adwords certification if you're so inclined to acquire one. As such I will not attempt to put years of knowledge into a single chapter of this guide. Instead, I'll provide you with a quick overview and recommendations on how to use Google Adwords to promote your local business. If you want to skip the explanation and dive right in, visit Adwords at https://www.google.com/ads.

First, let's give a quick example of Google Adwords in action. You'll notice a listing at the very top which is labeled as an "Ad". This

advertisement is appearing in this position because someone is running a Google Adwords campaign.

Considering that most people click on the first result or a result above the fold of the webpage after doing a search. Adding your listing in this position is an ideal way to attract new website visitors and potential customers.

How Google Adwords Functions

The way Adwords operates is pretty easy. In essence, it's an auction. You enter an amount that you are willing to pay per click each time someone clicks on your ad. If the amount you entered is higher than what other advertisers are willing to pay, and your ad is of good quality, it will generally appear higher in search results. If someone clicks on your ad and goes to your website or landing page, you'll pay the amount you entered or a price slightly higher than the next highest bidder. Aside from complex ranking algorithms, dynamic scoring, quality score, and pricing variations that we don't necessarily need to explore, the process is pretty straight forward.

Google also offers some campaigns that allow you to pay a fixed sum per 1,000 impressions, also called CPM or cost per thousand. This type of advertising is more akin to traditional advertising - buying an ad in a magazine and hoping someone calls you.

Personally I like to pay per click over impressions. Why pay for impressions when you can pay for actual visitors to your website or landing page? I'm not saying that the CPM model doesn't make sense. In fact, it works well for local Facebook advertising and 'remarketing' which we'll discuss later in this guide.

One of the good things about Google Adwords is you can create an ad campaign and almost immediately start receiving targeted traffic interested in your products or services. If you don't rank well for a search term in Google's natural results, Adwords offers a paid-for alternative to appear in search results alongside or above your closest competitors.

If you're new to Google Adwords, it's easy to become overwhelmed with the amount of options and statistics thrown at you, so it's best to focus on the basics before creating your first campaign. Also, just like Facebook and other advertising platforms, Google offers a local advertising option. It's not as targeted as creating a campaign from scratch but is certainly a viable option if you simply want to get started and have little or no online advertising expertise.

Before launching your Adwords campaign, consider these tips for crossing your "t"s and dotting your "i"s.

Tip #1: Start with a great website or landing page

A poor website or landing page can really hurt your Adwords campaign. Make sure all your website pages or landing pages, wherever you're sending traffic, load quickly and provide a strong call to action. You don't want to spend a ton of money generating traffic only to have peple bounce off your landing page. Make sure that all of the content on your page is relevant to the keywords you target.

A number of years ago, Google introduced something called a quality score. This measures the relevance of your page to the ads you're running. It also takes usability factors into consideration. If you produce a relevant, engaging landing page on your website or independently, Adwords will give you a higher quality score, reducing costs and improving average position.

Tip #2: Define your advertising goals

As a local business, its important to consider your online advertising goals. This is especially true if you're considering Adwords advertising for a particular niche. Adwords can be expensive so it behooves you to determine what you're willing to spend to acquire a new customer. My recommendation is to start with a modest budget, maybe $10/day. If you were to spend $300 this month on

advertising, what would you expect that to deliver for you? Alternatively, how many new clients would you have to generate at that cost to make a profit or reach a revenue goal.

By having a clear outcome in mind, you can determine what you're willing to spend to generate website traffic and how many prospects need to convert to paying customers. This math is extremely important. Where I see small businesses go wrong is when I hear them say, "I put $500 into Adwords and I didn't get a single sale." This is a bit misguided. Did you get clicks? What did those clicks cost? Did you test your landing page, your offer, your sales funnel? Work with a modest budget to begin and learn as you go. Measure your progress against specific advertising goals and keep at it until you start to see leads and sales.

Tip #3: Measure your campaign effectiveness

When launching a new campaign, set a fixed budget and watch your campaign closely. You need to give your Adwords campaign enough time to run, collect data, and help you make some informed decisions. Based on the type of Adwords campaign you've set up, this could take some time. For example, if you run an e-commerce website, success can be measured by how many people complete the checkout process. If you aren't selling products online, you'll need to track your results a different way such as how many people

called you, visited your store after learning about you online, or individuals filling out an inquiry form.

How will you measure success? Think in terms of conversions. A conversion needs to be some type of exchange from the prospect – an email, a signup, a call. Once you start receiving clicks and conversions, do the math. Can you justify the amount you're spending to generate new customers?

Tip #4: Learn the basics

It will benefit you greatly to become familiar with the basics of pay-per-click advertising. A clear understanding of definitions like CPC (cost per click), CTR (click through rate), impressions and conversions will be very helpful as you get started on the path of online advertising.

Within Adwords, Google provides a good number of videos that can help you learn more about Google Adwords, online advertising, and the numerous options they provide for generating local traffic for your business. I also recommend tha you check out Youtube or Udemy for inexpensive courses that can tell you everything you need to know about running high-performing Adwords campaigns.

As I mentioned earlier, Adwords does have a local advertising option. Personally I think this is a good way to start if you're new to online pay-per-click advertising. However, at some point, to get the true results you're looking for, you must grow your knowledge and expertise of Google Adwords advertising.

Lesson 16: Remarketing

Remarketing is a very powerful way to make the most of your local marketing dollars. One way to think about remarketing is to consider what happens when you stop into a car dealer and speak to a sales rep. He does everything to make sure you don't leave without buying a car but you insist, "I'm just looking, not quire ready to buy." After you leave the dealership, you start receiving phone calls and/or emails evert day from the rep until you either come back to the dealership and buy the car or finally respond to him and say, "I bought from someone else." A good friend of mine calls this the 'buy or die' method. Sorry, it's a dog eat dog world out there and if you're not selling to the prospect, someone else will. Here's how you can use remarketing to do the legwork or following up with potential customers in a completely automated way that's not as irritating as a daily phone call or email.

Remarketing

The process of remarketing begins when someone visits your website. Using Google AdWords remarketing, you place what's called a "pixel" onto your website pages that tags each person who visits. Once they've been "cookied", Google then shows your advertisement based on criteria you provided. When the individual visits other sites on the Google Ad network they see your static image, animated image, video or text ads.

What makes remarketing different from standard Display advertising is the targeting it provides. Remarketing consists of using a special tracking code to place cookies in the computer of people visiting your website, and then serves your ads to those with that cookie, specifically on the Display network.

The main point with remarketing is that you want to find those people who have shown enough interest in your products or services to visit your website. These people are more likely to convert than people who have not yet visited your website. There are a number of strategies for how to best target these people, which website visitors to target, how to make the most of your remarketing ads, and how to optimize these remarketing campaigns. According to some reasearch, users who have been targeted with

remarketing are 70% more likely to purchase than those who have not. So, if you're trying to increase conversions, remarketing is a great tool for doing so.

How to Put Remarketing Code on Your Website

There are two sets of code available for setting up AdWords remarketing. They are Google Analytics remarketing code and Adwords remarketing code. Remember that Google Analytics is tracking code for your website and Adwords is the advertising platform offered by Google. You can install these pieces of separate code on your own or use a freelancer to help you. If you've never installed tracking code on your website before, although it's easy to implement, I recommend you find a trusted freelancer who can implement the code for you.

Personally I use the Google Analytics remarketing code instead of AdWords because it also lets you use visitor behavior to target prosepcts. For example, you could create a list to target people in a certain geographical location who stayed on your website or visited certain pages or content. In contrast, the AdWords code only allows lists to be built based on pages viewed on your site which may not be as effective as more dynamic or two-dimensional targeting (geography plus behavior).

Once your code is placed, it's time to set up your campaign. As is true with any online marketing, there are a number of factors to consider before launching your remarketing campaign. The first factor to consider is called, "Duration". That is, how long do you want to continue marketing to your list through the Google Display Network?

Don't be a stalker!

It's tempting to choose the maximum list membership duration of 540 days but consider that most ordinary internet users won't be clearing their browser cookies. As a result, your ads will chase them across the internet for the full list duration unless they convert into a paying customer. Don't be a stalker! Through over exposure, you can turn prospects and even customers into people who have a negative image of your brand. Only set membership durations for as long as they're required. Set list duration on what you are trying to accomplish with your campaign. For example, if you are selling appliances, people usually start shopping for them within a few months of purchase, so don't chase them around for more than a 2 or 3 months. Most small businesses I work with have a 60 day window where they show ads and modify their exposure through a concept called frequency capping.

Frequency capping

One of most common questions I get is with regard to how frequently ads should be shown to those in your remarketing program.   Show them too frequently and you'll annoy your prospect. On the other hand, show your ads in just the right frequency over the right time and you can significantly improve website traffic and local in-store traffic.

To control your frequency capping, navigate to the Settings tab of your campaign, and set the cap at either the campaign, ad group or ad level. Choose whether to set it on monthly, weekly or daily limit as well. When deciding what level to set your frequency capping, consider how many remarketing campaigns you have, or how many ad groups there are within your remarketing campaign.

Assuming you have multiple campaigns, I'd recommend around two impressions per week, per campaign. This means that if you have five campaigns and a user is a member of at least one list in all the campaigns, the maximum exposure they would receive is 14 impressions per week. This is quite high, but the likelihood is that not all users will be on a list within each campaign, so the average frequency will be less.

Once your campaigns have been running a while and you have significant data, review reach and frequency data within the Dimensions tab. Here you can see how often visitors are served one of your remarketing ads and assess whether it's too often or frequency capping needs to be adjusted. When in doubt, review the data. Even with the best information, you'll have to make some assumptions. My motto is always be testing.

Improve Chances of Success

Here are a few things to consider when running an effective remarketing campaign. I've learned many of these things the hard way but they work. Consider the following:

Only target "quality" visitors. If you'd like to narrow down your remarketing so it only targets users who have had a quality interaction with your site, you could try adding specific criteria to your lists including the exclusion of people who visited your site and bounced off (no interaction with your content) and exclude people who have spent less than ten seconds on the site. This can be implemented by creating lists within Google Analytics and creating custom combination lists within AdWords which exclude them. Essentially you're creating a list in one system and telling the advertising system to exclude people on those lists.

Be selective about where you show your ads. There are some content types that you probably don't want your ads to show on. You can exclude site categories to avoid ads being shown around content that shouldn't be associated with your brand.

To exclude categories, access the Display Network Tab, scroll to the bottom of the page and click the green options button for campaigns. You will then exclude site categories. I recommend excluding error pages, parked domains and forums as these tend to have poor content that you may not want associated with your brand.

You can also experiment with excluding your ads from showing below the fold of the page to see how this affects performance. You should be aware that you may have to bid higher to ensure your ads are always eligible for above the-fold placement. Further refine your remarketing by reviewing your placement report and excluding any placements which aren't appropriate.

Make sure ad creative is relavent. For example, if you are trying to generate repeat purchases, your ad creative could contain a discount code for the consumer's next transaction. If you are targeting users who viewed a specific product page but didn't complete a purchase, your ad creative should feature that product.

Another thing to make sure of is that ad creative is similar to the look and feel of your website, include your logo, and bring users to a landing page that is not only appropriate but reflects your ad. The key here is to create a consistent and positive user experience.

Produce display ads of different sizes and test them all. Be sure to include a text ad in each ad group, as some sites won't support image ads and this ensures you'll have the opportunity to get in front of potential customers. You can always remove the text ad later if it performs poorly. Lastly, include a strong call to action on all of your ads. We want people clicking on your ads, not just veiwing them.

Remarketing Take-a-ways

Here are a few things to remember as you embark on remarketing for your local business. The goal here is to keep things simple while producing a result that helps you achieve your sales and marketing goals.

- Get started. Set up remarketing in Adwords and place your conversion tracking pixels
- Create remarketing lists
- Develop creative for each list (multipe sizes)

- Test your lists and custom combinations
- Exclude different categories (parked domains, forums, and other site categories)
- Test your landing pages

Remarketing as a concept is simple – place a pixel on your website and start targeting users with your ads once they leave in order to bring them back to your website or visit your business. The mechanics of remarketing can seem complicated if you've never run online advertising campaigns or specifically a remarketing campaign. That's why I recommend working with a freelancer or outsourcing partner who can do this work for you.

Lesson 17: Outsourcing

Trying to do everything in your business alone is a recipe for disaster. As your business grows, you need to think about regular activities that can be outsourced or subcontracted out. Some of the more popular outsourced activities include:

- Invoicing
- Accounting

- Marketing Services

When you can get assistance with things you probably aren't skilled at anyway, you'll have more time to focus on higher level activities like contacting customers, performing core services, or working on your business. In the beginning, you may not have the budget to hire all the staff you need or outsource all non-core activities, but there are a variety of options for leveraging freelancers to get things done cheaply and effectively.

Great leaders know that it's more productive to outsource work that is not revenue generating but essential to business operations. Since time is such an important commodity when running a local business, it's smart to leverage the talents of others rather than trying to do it yourself. Here are some of the best activities to outsource in your business.

Utilizing the right resources for finding freelancers and contract workers is essential. At the end of this section we'll show how to find the best and most affordable freelancers for outsourcing.

Subcontract Select Marketing Efforts: Marketing is the fuel of your business. As you're learning in this program, online local marketing efforts tie directly to your sales results. So if you're too busy working

in your business and need some help, considering outsourcing your local marketing efforts to a freelancer, consultant, or intern.

As long as you understand what needs to get done and how to do it, investing in someone to help execute can be money well spent. For example, some marketing people will help you develop downloadable content for your website, conduct email marketing campaigns, or manage your local directory submissions and updates. Some will focus on reaching out to LinkedIn contacts, handle direct inquiries, or pitch you for speaking opportunities. They can also develop media pitches and monitor local media opportunities.

Subcontract Your Social Media Marketing: There are plenty of solo-practitioners, marketing consultants, and social media marketing agencies that can handle developing your social media strategy, content development, and social promotion for your company. When you perform these tasks in-house you often fail to retain the consistency of doing them. Leverage the services of a freelancer to handle this for you. I am pretty sure, if you hire the right person or firm, and give them a specific niche focus and strong message about your product or service, your marketing efforts will flourish over time. Just remember that social media is a long-term strategy, so be prepared to invest 12-24 months to achieve your goals.

LOCAL MARKETING
MADE SIMPLE

Subcontract Your Administrative Support: Do you often feel like you wish you had another pair of hands to help you? Utilizing a virtual assistant or part-time help is a cost-effective way to get routine tasks handled in a business. You can use a virtual assistant for maintaining your personal schedule, database, preparing mailings, email newsletters, copy editing, blog maintenance, booking travel arrangements, invoicing, collections and voicemail and email management. I've used Twitter, LinkedIn, and Craigslist to search for qualified virtual assistants to support my business.

There's really no need to waste time and effort trying to do everything that needs to get done on your own. Even if you only subcontract one or two important tasks, the results will be extremely valuable. Be smart and choose reputable and recommended contractors. Do not sign any long-term contracts right away and begin with a one-to-three-month project. By outsourcing some non-core activities, you will have greater peace of mind as you help your business grow!

Resources

It took me many years to find the best resources for finding freelancers and contract workers to help with specific online

marketing and in-office projects. Here the best resources for finding what you need:

- **Upwork**

This site is the combination of two leaders in outsourcing (formerly eLance and Odesk) and is our go-to service for finding freelancers, virtual assistants, and companies willing to do project work. The benefit of using Upwork or a similar service includes: the size of the recruiting pool, your ability to evaluate candidates easily, and the process for safely managing projects and payments.

Work with someone perfect for your team

The process for finding a freelancer is simple. You begin by posting a description of the job you'd like completed, what you are willing to pay, and how long the position is for. Once posted, you will receive multiple offers. Simply review available contractors and select the

one you want. You will then set up milestones, fund your account, and begin.

Payments: Pay your freelancer per hour or per project, whichever you choose. For hourly projects, the freelancer bills you once a week and Upwork sends a secure payment to your freelancer. For fixed-price projects, Upwork releases funds to your freelancer after they meet pre-set milestones. In either case, you're covered by the Upwork Payment Protection program, assuring that you only pay for work you approve.

All payments go through their secure system and you can choose from the following billing methods:

- Credit card
- PayPal
- Bank account

When they send your payments to the freelancer, they deduct a 10% fee from the rate they charge you. For example, if you pay your freelancer $20, they earn $18 and Upwork receives $2.

Protection: Upwork offers some great tools giving you visibility into work the freelancer is doing. This includes:

- Work Diary. This tool captures snapshots of your freelancer's screen every 10 minutes, helping to verify that on hourly jobs, work has been completed as invoiced.

- Payment Protection. Upwork Payment Protection assures you that you pay only for work you've approved.

- Dispute Resolution. If an issue ever should arise, Upwork has programs to help fix the situation.

- Freelancer

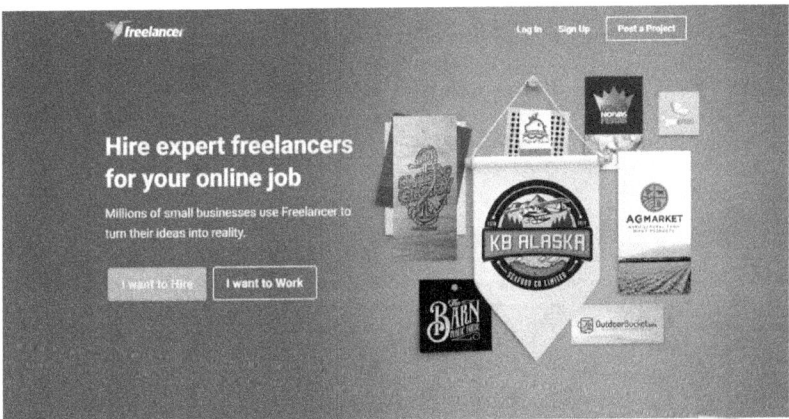

This is another great sit for finding freelancers that can do just about anything related to your business marketing and support functions. Finding a freelancer works much the same way on this site as Upwork. Register, post your project, and view freelancer profiles.

- Get bids from skilled freelancers in minutes.

- View freelancer profiles and feedback, then instantly chat with them.

- With only a 3% commission fee, your favorite freelancer can start working for you quickly.

- Pay the freelancer once you're 100% satisfied. Minimum fees may apply if work is cancelled.

Consider Freelancer.com after you have tried Upwork. Although the website platforms are similar, I have found Upwork to have more of the technical and creative resources needed for effective online marketing, web development, and other technical functions.

- ## Fiverr

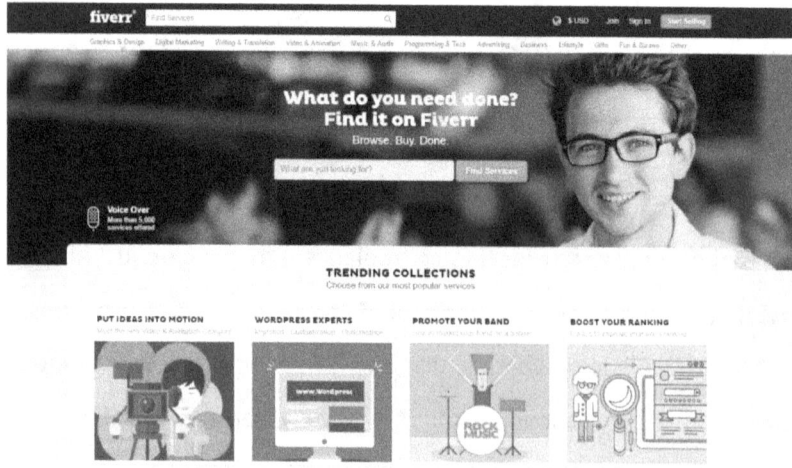

If you need something done, a small task like design, transcription, video production, etc., then Fiverr is a great resource. The platform is composed of people who are good at specific tasks and looking to complete work. Fiverr is a secure platform that gives you access to a variety of individual providers on the cheap. Although most "gigs" are advertised at $5, you'll probably want to add extras so expect to spend around $25 on average.

Hiring a freelancer has never been easier thanks to these amazing resources for marketing, web development, or administrative work. In addition to finding freelancers for local online marketing, there are other sources you can use for back office functions and even finding resources to build your team.

Lesson 18: Lessons Learned

In this section we'll explore some of the most important things you can do and not do in order to accelerate your Online local marketing. These strategies are proven to increase your online presence and drive targeted leads to your practice.

- **Local Marketing Do's:**

Optimize your website for mobile: Make it easy for customers and followers who use mobile devices, tablets and Smartphones when accessing your website. Smartphone and tablet users use their mobile devices two to six times in a week to search local businesses. Additionally, Google penalizes websites who are not optimized for mobile devices.

Provide Accurate Information: Always keep your online information accurate, updated, and accessible throughout the web and on all publisher's listings. Having accurate, up-to-date information about your business is essential. Updating the information on a regular basis and consistent is important for maintaining top organic rankings.

Offer High Quality Content: Your website content should be impressive and useful for customers. Have helpful information, including FAQs about your services will make it easy for your customers to be educated about your business and leave reviews. Quality content and effective reviews leave a good impression on your customers while positively impacting your search engine ranking.

Update your profile: You should update your business profile from time to time with updated images, new product or services

offerings. Search engines love consistency but they also want to display the most current search results.

Include multi-media: Dynamic content such as videos and images increase your appeal in local marketing efforts. This additional content is ideal for search engines and can boost your business rankings. Video for example has a much higher engagement rate and will stand out in search results.

You can include customers' testimonials, product demonstrations and customer service staff in your videos and images to make them more powerful.

Correctly optimize webpages: On-page SEO is associated with page title, URL, header tags, image alt text, and page content. You can consider the geographic area in which you provide service, including suburbs or nearby towns. For an in-depth look at developing a well-optimized website check out SEO Made Simple.

You can optimize webpages by integrating keywords, specific service language, and content that describes your business and the area you service with a consistent NAP (name, address and Phone) listing on online directories. This helps local web browsers easily find your business.

Stand Out: You should always try to be different from other local businesses and service providers in order to stand out from the crowd. Be sure to tell your audience what you are providing that competitors don't and why you're the clear choice. This gives them a clear reason to be serviced by you.

Utilize ambassadors: Social media pages work as your brand ambassador. Some people check their Facebook account more often than their mailbox. You can create mini pages to drive your traffic to your business blog or simply utilize the social platforms to get more traffic. Create well optimized social media accounts and actively manage them in a meaningful way.

Use strong calls to action: When it comes to lead generation, through your website, online advertising or email, always include a strong call to action. You can run an introductory offer, free trial, % off on products, etc. People always look for offers and discounts. With this type of approach, you can get a great deal of traffic to your website, keeping your funnel full with prospects.

Claim your Profile: You can list your business in local directories either individually or using a data aggregator. Each directory serves different purposes, but overall they increase your visibility on the web.

You can claim your business on Google Places, Yelp, Manta, and others. As noted earlier in this program, using a data aggregator or local marketing provider is a great way to increase your online visibility across multiple local directories quickly, easily, and affordably over a sustained period of time. Don't set and forget.

Think like your customers: Walking in your customer's shoes will be one of the greatest things you can do for a successful local marketing program. You must think like a prospect or customer to really understand your business and why someone should do business with you.

- What makes you unique?

- What makes someone confidence in their choice to use you?

- What type of brand do you have?

- What kind of experience does a prospect have when they fill out an inquiry or call your office?

- What's their in-office experience like?

- Do you follow up and communicate with them on a regular and personal basis?

- What other options are they seeing online and how do you stack up?

All of these factors must be considered from the perspective of someone who may need your products or services in the local area. It will change the way you approach your online local marketing, your messaging, offers, etc.

Be sure to review this list of "Do's" and make sure you understand and implement them. Once you have a handle on what to do, focus on what not to do...

- **Local Marketing "Do Not's":**

Don't Create Fake Reviews: Do not write fake reviews for your business. I know this is tempting, but search engines are getting better at detecting fake reviews. If you post fake reviews you could face a penalty that harms your business' local search engine ranking for a long time. Instead, set up a computer in the office to collect online reviews or simply ask those providing positive feeback to leave a review on Google+ (send them a link and make it really easy for them to do so).

Don't Spam prospects or customers: Just because you have someone's contact information doesn't mean you send them emails

every hour, day, or week. If you do so, customers will unsubscribe from your list forever. The goal of your email communications should be to inform, connect, or advance prospects and customers through the purchase decision funnel.

Don't set it and forget it: Remember things change on the web and you must keep an eye on all the changes happening in local marketing. For example, the Google algorithm changes regularly as well as social media and online marketing tools. Stay on top of your local online marketing efforts, driving more leads to your business and effectively converting them to customers.

Don't Use P.O. Box Address: If you use a P.O. Box address for your business, it will be difficult for search engines to determine where your local business is located geographically. As a result, Google will not allow verification of your Google My Business listing. If you run your business in your own home, then you should always use your physical address as your business address. If this is an issue, consider renting a mailbox from a virtual mailbox provider.

Don't focus only on new customers: You should appeal to both new and existing customers. New customers are usually most interested in your contact information and back ground unlike existing

customers who are often interested more in your services, discounts, and new offers.

Don't rely only on Search Engine traffic alone: Local people don't just use Google to find businesses around their local area. Although online local search is the primary way people find local businesses today, many also utilize social media, review sites, recommendations, and referrals. Make sure your online local marketing supports all of these touch points.

Don't over optimize: Search Engine Optimization is important, but do not try to over optimize your website. Search engines penalize those who try to game the system with keyword stuffing and other "blackhat" SEO techniques. Try to optimize for targeted keywords that users are searching for.

Don't use a toll-free number: Although toll-free telephone numbers used to be all the rage, today they will make it difficult for the search engines to find your geographic location.

Don't ignore Negative Reviews: Negative reviews are a great opportunity to learn about a customer's perspective regarding your services. No one expects every business to be perfect, but they do expect you to be fair and kind. Be responsive to people who offer

Negative Reviews, thank them for being honest, and respond to their concerns.

Wrap Up

I'm thrilled that you have chosen to learn more about local online marketing for your business and I wish you amazing success. If you enjoyed this guide, I have something that can help you further. This information is also available in my online training program, covering similar topics and expanded information about effective online marketing. I invite you to get the most out of Local Marketing by learning more about our online program and additional local marketing resources.

Thanks so much for the time you have dedicated to learning how to get the most advantages from Local Marketing. Local Marketing is here to stay!

See you at the top,

Michael H. Fleischner

BONUS: Visit http://LocalMarketingMadeSimple.com for bonuses, audio downloads, and course information.

www.ingramcontent.com/pod-product-compliance
Lightning Source LLC
Chambersburg PA
CBHW060349190526
45169CB00002B/538